cool science

Life on the Edge

Cherie Winner

LERNER PUBLICATIONS COMPANY
MINNEAPOLIS

The author thanks Dr. Kevin Humphries,
head of the forensics lab of the Colorado
Bureau of Investigation, for sharing his
knowledge and enthusiasm.

Text copyright © 2006 by Cherie Winner

All rights reserved. International copyright secured. No part of this book may be reproduced, stored in a retrieval system, or transmitted in any form or by any means—electronic, mechanical, photocopying, recording, or otherwise—without the prior written permission of Lerner Publishing Group, except for the inclusion of brief quotations in an acknowledged review.

Lerner Publications Company
A division of Lerner Publishing Group
241 First Avenue North
Minneapolis, Minnesota 55401 U.S.A.

Website address: www.lernerbooks.com

Library of Congress Cataloging-in-Publication Data

Winner, Cherie.
        Life on the edge / by Cherie Winner.
            p.   cm. — (Cool science)
        Includes bibliographical references and index.
        ISBN-13: 978–0–8225–2499–1 (lib. bdg. : alk. paper)
        ISBN-10: 0–8225–2499–6 (lib. bdg. : alk. paper)
        1. Adaptation (Biology)—Juvenile literature. 2. Extreme environments—Juvenile literature. I. Title.
    II. Series.
    QH546.W56 2006
    578.75′8—dc22   2005011071

Manufactured in the United States of America
1 2 3 4 5 6 – BP – 11 10 09 08 07 06

Table of Contents

Introduction

One of the biggest mysteries in science is whether we are alone in the universe. Is Earth the only planet that harbors life? Since the 1960s, the United States and other nations have sent probes to nearby planets and beyond.

In 2004 robotic rovers began searching Mars for signs of life. Another mission scanned Titan, one of Saturn's moons. By the time you read this, we might know whether these distant worlds are as dead as they look. We may discover whether they're home to organisms that thrive in environments we never thought could support life.

The Mars rover *Opportunity* made ring patterns (*above*) where it took samples of the planet's soil in 2004. Scientists think extreme organisms may have once lived on Mars—and maybe still do.

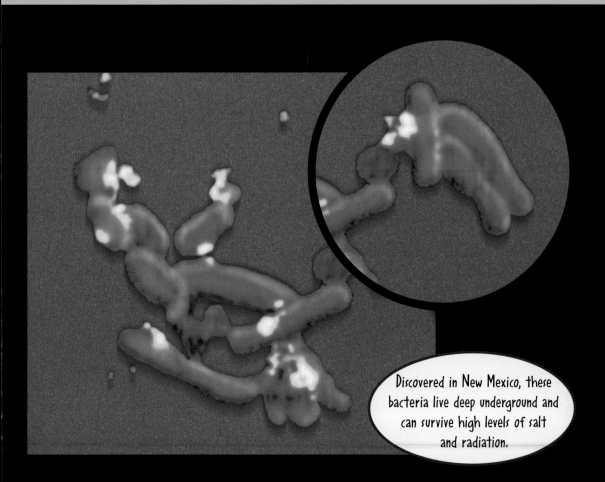

Discovered in New Mexico, these bacteria live deep underground and can survive high levels of salt and radiation.

Of course, extreme environments don't exist only on other planets. Many places on Earth are so cold, hot, smelly, or toxic that nothing could possibly live there. Or could it? As nasty as these environments seem to us, scientists have found that they are home to thousands of organisms. Some extreme environments host many kinds of living things—animals, plants, and microbes. (Microbes are organisms so small we need a microscope to see them.) Other environments are so severe that only a few microbes can survive there.

Scientists have discovered many of these special creatures very recently. But they're already finding ways to put these critters to work. Extreme organisms are helping us identify criminals, clean up sewage, and get our stonewashed jeans just the right shade of blue.

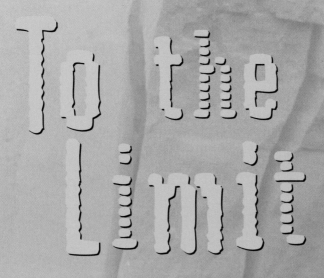

chapter 1

To the Limit

What do scientists mean when they talk about an "extreme environment"? How bad can it be?

Think of a setting that makes you miserable—searing summer heat, icy winter wind, the stench from an industrial plant, or a pile of rotting garbage. Then picture something much, much worse. Imagine living in a pool of boiling hot water, clinging to a snow-covered rock in Antarctica. Or think about being stuck in a pile of toxic sludge that could burn a hole in concrete.

All extreme organisms, or extremophiles (eks-TREEM-oh-files), have one thing in common. They've figured out how to survive in conditions that would kill almost every other creature on the planet. They don't avoid the bad stuff, like birds that fly south when the weather gets cold. Extreme organisms live in their hostile habitat full-time.

Why Bother?

If extreme environments are so bad, why does anything bother to live in them? Wouldn't it be easier to stay in a coral reef, grassy meadow, or lush jungle?

Yes, in some ways it would be easier. But life on the edge has a few advantages. "Normal" places are crowded. A meadow or jungle is home to millions of animals and plants, and billions of microbes. Living there means competing with all those neighbors for food, water, space, and light, and putting up with predators that try to eat you. On the other hand, if you live in an extreme environment, you have the place almost all to yourself.

FUN FACT!

Biologists name extreme organisms for the kind of environment they like and then add *phile,* from a Greek word meaning "loving." All organisms that live in extreme environments are extremophiles. Those that love heat are thermophiles, those that love acid are acidophiles, and so on.

Antarctica's frozen landscape (*above*) may not look like a good place to live. But a few birds, fish, plants, and microbes make their homes there.

Besides, what seems extreme to us is normal to these creatures. The nasty conditions that keep other organisms out offer extremophiles just what they need. In fact, most extreme organisms die if they're brought to a "normal" environment. To them, the world *we* live in is extreme—and deadly.

Long, Long Ago

Life first appeared on Earth between 3.5 and 4 billion years ago. Earth then was a very different place than it is now. It was much hotter. The atmosphere contained almost no oxygen and gave little protection against ultraviolet rays from the Sun. We could not have survived in such an environment. Neither could most animals or plants.

But some organisms thrived on the early Earth. Over time, Earth cooled. The planet gained an atmosphere rich in oxygen.

This artwork shows how scientists think Earth looked millions of years ago. Early Earth was much too extreme for humans.

Life Is Everywhere

Almost every place we used to think was lifeless is teeming with life. New species are discovered every week. Each has an unusual ability suited to its extreme environment. More than one hundred species of bacteria have been found living in radioactive soil at a nuclear waste dump. A snail that

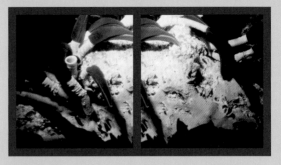

These tube worms live deep in the ocean in nearly total darkness.

lives at the bottom of the Indian Ocean makes armor for itself out of iron in the water. Worms named *Osedax* grow greenish "roots" that attach to the bones of dead whales that have sunk to the bottom of the ocean.

The extreme habitats shrank. Organisms similar to Earth's first organisms still live in scattered places. Some are on the surface. Others lie at the bottom of the ocean or deep underground. These harsh habitats are safe places for organisms that need their extreme conditions to live.

The World of Microbes

Some extremophiles are close relatives of animals such as birds, fish, and insects. Others are microbes—organisms that we need a microscope to see. Many familiar microbes are types of bacteria. Bacteria are single-celled organisms. They may be round or rod-shaped. But most bacteria, like most animals, do not live in extreme environments.

Archaea (ar-KEY-uh), another kind of microbe, look a lot like bacteria. But they are not closely related. In fact, most archaea aren't even closely related to each other. Two species of archaea that live in the same drop of water may be genetically more different from each other than you are from a rattlesnake or a redwood tree. Most archaea are extremophiles.

A few extremophiles are single-celled fungi. These plantlike organisms include molds, mushrooms, and the yeast used to make bread. Not all fungi are extremophiles.

In the coming chapters, we'll take a tour of a few of Earth's harshest habitats to find out exactly how these amazing extremophiles live. Let's start our safari in Yellowstone National Park—home to some microbes that really cook!

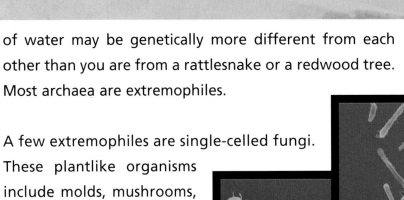

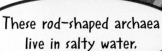
These rod-shaped archaea live in salty water.

chapter 2

Hot and Cold

The thermal pools (hot springs) in Yellowstone National Park look inviting, with vivid greens, gleaming golds, and dazzling blues. But don't touch! The pools hold incredibly hot water that can kill curious visitors.

Yellowstone's thermal pools hold fascinating life-forms, but scientists couldn't prove this for many years. Scientists would collect a sample of hot pool water and take it to their lab. There they would add nutrients to the sample and let it sit for a few days to see if it contained any microbes. In the process, they cooled the water sample to room temperature.

FUN FACT!

Yellowstone Park isn't the only spot on Earth with thermal pools. You'll also find them in countries such as New Zealand, Japan, Iceland, and Italy. They form wherever water flows to the surface after being heated by volcanic action deep underground. Most thermal pools that scientists have studied contain thermophiles.

Scientists never imagined that cooling down might kill the hot pool microbes. But it did. Thermophiles love heat but can't handle "normal" temperatures at all.

Then, in the 1960s, biologist Thomas Brock tried keeping his samples as hot as the pool where he collected them. He discovered a whole world of tiny organisms in the steaming water. One of Brock's heat-loving microbes was a bacterium he called *Thermus aquaticus*. Its name means "living in hot water." It was the first organism ever found that lives at temperatures up to 176°F (80°C). Other microbes Brock found were archaea, a form of life scientists had rarely seen before.

Butter and Eggs

Why are thermophiles at home in very hot places? And why can't other forms of life survive in them? A lot of things can go wrong when ordinary cells get too hot. Two of the biggest problems involve membranes and proteins.

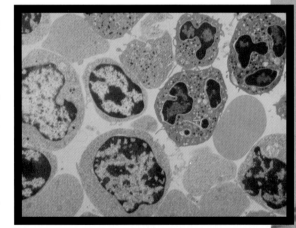

Every cell is surrounded by a membrane that keeps *in* materials the cell needs. It keeps *out* materials that shouldn't enter the cell. Membranes are made of fats. They get soft and leaky when they're heated, just like a glob of butter on really hot toast.

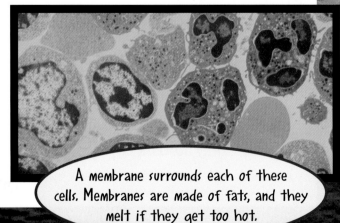

A membrane surrounds each of these cells. Membranes are made of fats, and they melt if they get too hot.

When this happens, the membranes no longer form a barrier between the inside of the cell and the outside. The cell dies.

Heat hurts a cell's proteins too. Proteins are the tiny building blocks of all cells. They start out as long chains. Then they fold up into just the right shape to do their job. But if they get too hot, they unfold. They stick to each other and stop working right. These proteins can damage or kill cells.

By cooking an egg, you can see what happens when proteins get too hot. When you break open an egg, the raw egg white is clear and jiggly. The white's proteins are folded up in their normal shapes. As the egg cooks, the proteins unfold and stick together. The clear, jiggly material turns white and becomes more solid. Something similar happens when living cells get too hot. Once their proteins have unfolded, they can't fold up the right way again, even if the temperature drops. You can't uncook an egg!

A cooked egg (top) looks different than an uncooked egg (bottom). Heating an egg changes its proteins and makes them stick together.

Thermophiles also have a special set of proteins, called heat shock proteins (HSPs). These proteins protect them from heat damage. HSPs prevent other proteins from losing their shape when heated. Most living things make HSPs only when they're overheated. Thermophiles seem to make them all the time.

Some thermophile proteins don't need HSPs to protect them from heat. All cells have special proteins called enzymes that speed up chemical reactions. Thermophile enzymes work at very high temperatures. Scientists can use these "thermo-zymes" for experiments that work best in high heat.

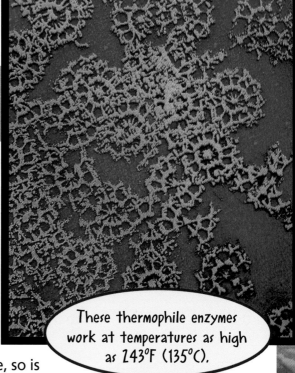

These thermophile enzymes work at temperatures as high as 243°F (135°C).

Catching the Crooks

The most famous example of a thermo-zyme at work is DNA (deoxyribonucleic acid) profiling. Police use DNA profiling to compare the genetic material of a suspected criminal with genetic material from a crime scene. Just as the pattern of each person's fingerprints is unique, so is the pattern of each person's DNA.

DNA profiling uses a thermo-zyme called Taq polymerase (tack poh-LIM-er-ase). Taq polymerase came from Brock's old friend, *Thermus aquaticus*. (The name *Taq* comes from the first letters of both names.) In 1983 another scientist, Kary Mullis, figured out how to use it to quickly make thousands of copies of a sample of DNA. He invented polymerase chain reaction (PCR). Other researchers used this process to turn a tiny bit of DNA from a crime scene into a sample big enough to identify. Ten years later, Mullis won the Nobel Prize in Chemistry for his polymerase work.

A scientist compares DNA samples. The Taq polymerase enzyme has made DNA profiling much faster than it used to be.

In thermophiles, Taq polymerase helps copy DNA when cells divide. Before it was discovered, crime labs needed to start with large samples of genetic material to create a DNA profile. And they had to wait three to six months before they had their test results.

But sometimes police find only a tiny speck of DNA at a crime scene. With Taq polymerase, police can make billions of copies of that speck. This gives police a large enough sample to compare the DNA with other samples. Making the copies happens at high temperatures. It's important that the enzyme used isn't damaged by heat. Taq polymerase is fast. Within two weeks, police know whether their suspect was at the scene of the crime.

Scientists have also used Taq polymerase to make other experiments with DNA faster and easier. It even helped scientists figure out the way that human DNA is arranged. That's quite an achievement for a heat-loving microbe that nobody even knew existed a few decades ago!

What Is DNA?

Deoxyribonucleic acid is a chemical that carries the instructions that tell a cell what proteins to make. It's like a blueprint containing all the information the cell or organism will need to survive. In fungi, plants, and animals, the DNA is in the nucleus (central part) of each cell. Bacteria and archaea don't have a nucleus. Their DNA mixes with all the other chemicals in the cell.

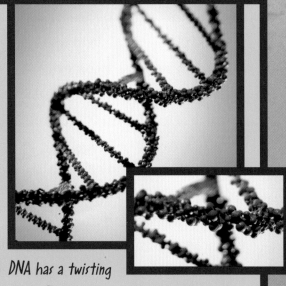

DNA has a twisting shape. This shape is called a double helix.

And Some Like It Cold

After visiting some of the hottest spots on Earth, let's take a quick tour of some of the coldest. Far away from Yellowstone's bubbling pools, microbes cling to an icy ledge in Antarctica. In the sea below them, fish cruise through water that is actually colder than freezing.

Some organisms survive cold times by becoming dormant. Like a bear that hibernates or a tree that sheds its leaves, these organisms don't become active until the environment warms up. True psychrophiles (SY-crow-files), or cold-loving organisms, don't wait for the cold to end. They can't live without it. If you put them at room temperature, they die.

Chilling Out

Nearly three hundred species of fish live in the ocean surrounding Antarctica. It's a tough assignment. The water around them is about 28°F (–2°C)—below the freezing point of their blood.

If a fish's body fluids freeze, its cells can't perform the chemical reactions that keep the fish alive. Another problem is that water expands when it freezes. Have you ever left a can of pop in the freezer overnight and had it explode? Just imagine what happens when ice forms in a fish's heart!

Freezing can happen in a flash. If one ice crystal forms in a fish's body, others can form around it in an explosion of crystallization. That's bad news for polar fish, because ice crystals float in the water all around them.

Polar fish protect themselves from freezing with antifreeze proteins (AFPs) in their body. AFPs lower the freezing point of a fish's blood by a couple of degrees—just enough to let the fish keep swimming in its frigid environment. Different kinds of fish make AFPs that work in different ways. The AFP made by winter flounder forms a spiral. It binds to ice crystals that start to form inside the fish's body and keeps them from spreading.

FUN FACT!
The ocean's saltiness is the reason that seawater is still liquid below 32°F (0°C), which is the freezing point of water. Seawater freezes at a lower temperature than freshwater. The more salt, the lower the freezing point is.

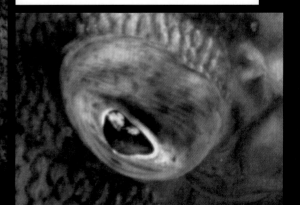

Winter flounder (below) produce antifreeze proteins called AFPs. AFPs allow the fish to live in frigid waters.

Enzymes and Membranes

Polar fish and other psychrophiles have special enzymes that work best at low temperatures. Their membranes also stay flexible in the cold.

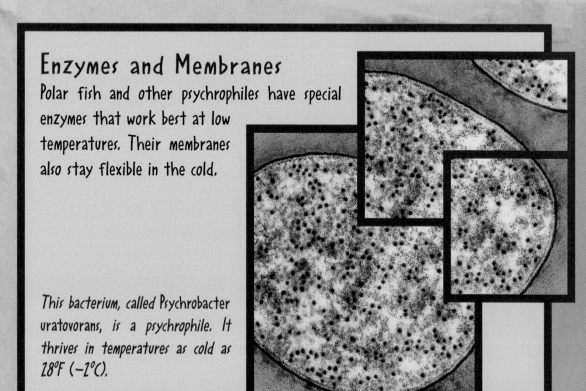

This bacterium, called Psychrobacter uratovorans, is a psychrophile. It thrives in temperatures as cold as 28°F (−2°C).

Putting AFPs to Work

Polar fish make AFPs because their DNA has genes that tell the fish's cells to create AFPs. Some scientists are trying to put the genes for AFPs into plants that normally don't survive in cold weather. These scientists, called genetic engineers, experiment with the genes of many different organisms. If they succeed, we may one day have oranges that can't be killed by an early frost. Maybe we'll even grow banana trees in Alaska!

One of the very coolest applications of AFPs is in ice-cream technology. Have you ever opened a container of ice cream and then left it in your freezer for a few months? When you took it out of the freezer again, the top of the ice cream was probably covered with big ice crystals. Proteins from psychrophiles can prevent that from happening. If no ice crystals form, your ice cream stays creamier longer. And that's a delicious scientific breakthrough!

chapter 3

Deep Secrets

Oceans cover about three-quarters of Earth's surface. Near the poles, they are extreme environments because they are so cold. But the polar oceans aren't the weirdest habitats in salt water. Deep below the surface, scientists have found some of the most extreme environments on Earth—environments we're just beginning to learn about.

Scratching the Surface

Would you believe that scientists know more about the Moon than about the deep ocean? It's true. We had good maps of the Moon years before we mapped the ocean floor. We've sent humans to the Moon six times but to the ocean's deepest point only once.

In 1960 ocean explorers Don Walsh and Jacques Piccard rode the stubby submarine *Trieste* to the Challenger Deep. That's the deepest point in the ocean. It's in the Mariana Trench, a long gash in the floor

How does the highest spot on Earth compare to the lowest? If you could pick up Mount Everest (Earth's tallest mountain) and turn it upside down, it would fit inside the Mariana Trench—and still be covered by more than 1 mile (1.6 km) of water.

of the western Pacific Ocean. There, almost 7 miles (11 kilometers) down, they saw a flatfish slide past their little ship. Unfortunately, Walsh and Piccard couldn't stay long enough to look for more sea creatures.

No one has ever repeated this journey. It's too dangerous and too expensive. You probably have a better chance of someday going to Mars than of visiting the Challenger Deep.

Mega Pressure

The biggest problem for ocean explorers is the incredible pressure underwater. The deeper you go, the greater the weight of water around you. In the Challenger Deep, you'd feel about 16,000 pounds per square inch (1,100 kilograms per square centimeter) of pressure. To get an idea what that might feel like, here's 1 square inch.

1 square inch

Imagine the whole weight of a huge male elephant on that space. Add another elephant on the inch next to that and a third elephant on the inch next to that and so on. Can you say squish?

Deep-sea creatures don't have a problem with the pressure around them. They balance the ocean's pressure by having equal pressure inside. All of us have pressure inside our bodies that balances the pressure from our surroundings. When our pressure and the outside pressure balance, we don't even notice it. If you went into outer space without a protective suit, your pressure inside would be so much greater than the pressure outside that you would explode. That's what happens to deep-sea organisms when they are brought to the surface.

Since we can't bring very many critters to the surface, we have to find ways to study them in their natural habitat. Scientists can ride research subs in areas where the ocean floor isn't too deep. The research sub *Alvin* could travel 2.8 miles (4.5 km) below the surface. To reach areas deeper than that, we explore by remote control. Remote operated vehicles (ROVs) are robotic submarines built to take incredible amounts of pressure. They have video cameras, temperature probes, mechanical arms, and sample chambers.

A crew on the deep-sea submarine *Alvin* (*above*) explores the ocean in 1978. A robotic ROV (*left*) doesn't carry any passengers. It can dive deeper than most manned submarines.

When this tripod fish touches the ocean floor with its long, bony rays (arrows), it will be at just the right height to snag shrimp that swim by.

In the Dark

Darkness is another challenge for animals in the deep ocean. At the ocean bottom, you can't see any glimmer of sunlight even when you look up at the surface! Each species that lives in these murky depths has its own way of surviving.

The graceful tripod fish has long, bony rays that stick out below its tail fin and both pectoral (chest) fins. When the fish "stands" with its long rays on the ocean floor, it can get dinner without even seeing its meal. The tripod fish's mouth ends up at just the right height to catch shrimp and tiny fish swimming by!

As for finding a mate, tripod fish have it covered. Each individual has male and female parts. If two tripod fish happen to meet, they mate.

But if a tripod fish doesn't find a partner, it makes both sperm and eggs to produce offspring all by itself.

Hidden Gardens

The richest habitats in the deep ocean are around hydrothermal vents. A vent is like an underwater spout where superhot water and dissolved minerals spew out of Earth's crust. The high pressure at the ocean bottom lets water stay liquid (instead of turning into steam) at far hotter temperatures than its normal boiling point of 212°F (100°C). Water comes out of the vents at 570°F to 750°F (300°C to 400°C)! It cools off when it mixes with the chilly seawater. But the area around the vent becomes a cozy home for animals that can't live on colder parts of the ocean floor.

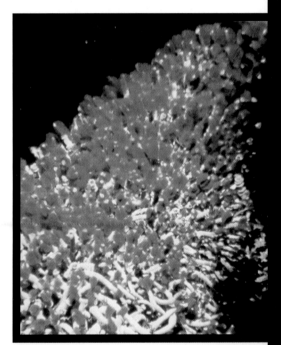

When the hot minerals coming out of the vent hit the cold water of the surrounding ocean, they become solid. Over time they pile up to form spouts called chimneys, or black smokers. One chimney off the coast of Oregon is more than 150 feet (46 meters) tall! It's known as Godzilla.

Tube worms cluster at the base of a black smoker. The hot vent provides a warm home for the worms and many other extremophiles.

Hotter Than Hot Springs

Vent microbes thrive at temperatures around 230°F to 248°F (110°C to 120°C)—much hotter than Yellowstone's hot springs. Biologists call these microbes hyperthermophiles. Many hyperthermophiles feed on the minerals coming out of the vent.

Bacteria (blue) cluster on the skin of worms (yellow) near a hot vent.

One animal lives right on the chimneys, where superhot water rushes out. It's the Pompeii (pom-PAY) worm, named for an ancient Roman city that was destroyed by a volcano. The Pompeii worm is the most heat-tolerant animal on Earth. With its tail next to the chimney and its head sticking out into the water, the worm builds a papery tube around itself. That's where it stays its whole life, surrounded by dozens of other Pompeii worms in their little tubes.

To measure the temperature of a Pompeii worm, Craig Cary and his research team designed a temperature probe called the Mosquito. It's small, it works in high pressure, and it fits on the end of a remote-controlled arm. From his seat inside *Alvin*, Cary guided the Mosquito into a Pompeii worm's tube. He has found that the head of the worm is about 72°F (22.2°C). Its hind end reaches 176°F (80°C). That's the biggest known difference in temperature across the body of any animal.

You thought the ocean was salty? Just watch as we head to bodies of water in which every drop is so salty, you can't even choke it down.

chapter 4

Not a Drop to Drink

Welcome to the world of salt lakes. These lakes are so salty that even ocean creatures can't live in them. A few organisms have figured out how to live in these conditions, though. The Dead Sea, located in the Middle East between Israel and Jordan, is one of the saltiest lakes on Earth. It's about eight times saltier than seawater. Despite its name, even the Dead Sea has life in it.

All living things need some salt, but too much is deadly. If salt gets into cells, it gums up the proteins. If it stays outside, it pulls so much water out of the cells that they die of dehydration—even in the middle of a lake. Organisms that live in salt lakes have solved both of these problems. They have pumps in their membranes that push out salt. Special molecules inside their cells that keep water in.

As if all that salt weren't bad enough, many salt lakes are also alkaline (AL-kuh-lin), or soda. Chemically, alkaline is the opposite of acid. But to

FUN FACT!

Both acids and alkalis, or bases, can sting or burn. Vinegar and lemon juice are acids. Battery acid is one of the strongest acids known. Drain cleaner and bleach are very strong bases.

living things, it's just as nasty. And yet a few organisms thrive in soda lakes. We use an enzyme from one of them to dye denim for that stonewashed look.

Eating Out

Salt-loving critters are called halophiles (HAY-low-files). The world's most famous halophiles are probably the brine shrimp in Utah's Great Salt Lake. Brine shrimp are sold as fish food and "sea monkeys."

For years, brine shrimp had the lake to themselves. It was too salty for predators.

Brine shrimp thrive in the waters of a salt lake. They can survive in very salty water that is deadly to other organisms.

The Dead Sea is one of Earth's saltiest lakes. The white areas in this photo are clumps of salt.

Since the mid-1990s, the Great Salt Lake has become less salty. This change was caused by extra snow in the nearby mountains. When the snow melted, an unusually large amount of water flowed into the lake. That diluted the salt enough for other animals to live there. Powerful insects called water boatmen moved into the lake. They glide across the water and devour brine shrimp by the millions.

Try It for Yourself

To taste how salty these lakes are, try this. Pour 1 cup (240 ml.) of freshwater into a glass. Stir in 1.5 teaspoons (10 grams) of table salt. Take a sip. That's like seawater. Now stir in another tablespoon (20 grams) of salt. Taste again. Pretty bad, huh? To make it as salty as the Dead Sea, you'd have to add 3 *more* tablespoons (60 grams) of salt!

Spirulina (left) is a halophile that lives in soda lakes. It often clumps together in piles along the shores of these lakes *(above)*.

People eat halophiles too. Bacteria called *Spirulina* live in soda lakes in Africa and Central America. Spirulina are sometimes called blue green algae. But blue green algae are really bacteria that look a lot like algae. Some lakes have so much *Spirulina* that mounds of it pile up along the shore. People gather it, dry it to a powder, and make high-protein biscuits out of it. Health food stores in the United States also sell dried *Spirulina*. Oh yum, pond scum!

High-Tech Halophiles

Halophiles make one of the coolest proteins ever discovered. It has a tongue-twister name, bacteriorhodopsin (back-TEER-ee-oh-roh-DOP-sin). When bacteriorhodopsin is exposed to light, the protein creates an electrical charge. That provides the energy it needs to keep salt out of the cell.

The electrical charge is very small—much too small to turn on a light bulb. But bacteriorhodopsin has another talent. When it is exposed to light, it changes shape and color. Computer scientists are inventing ways to use bacteriorhodopsin in programs that let computers recognize faces. They're even making bioelectric computers. These computers use both bacteriorhodopsin and semiconductors, miniature electronic devices that run most computers.

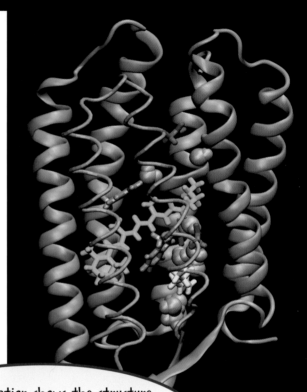

This illustration shows the structure of the bacteriorhodopsin. The protein converts light into an electrical charge, which keeps salt out of halophile cells.

chapter 5

Down in the Dirt

When two cavers stepped into Romania's Movile Cave in 1988, they entered an alien world. The limestone cave had been sealed off for more than five million years. Its creatures had evolved without any contact with the outside world. The life in the cave was so bizarre that it could have come from another planet.

Go Eat a Rock

So far, biologists have found more than thirty species of animals in Movile Cave that live nowhere else. They include eyeless spiders, transparent crabs, wingless flies, and worm-sucking leeches. The food that fuels these animals is equally unusual. Some of the cave creatures eat each other, but what about the rest? The cave receives no sunlight, it doesn't have plants, and it doesn't get nutrients from outside.

So where do the nutrients come from? From the rock itself. In Movile

This eyeless spider lives in Romania's Movile Cave. The cave is completely dark. The spider must use its senses of smell and touch to find its way around and to hunt.

Cave, rock-eating microbes are the first link in the food chain. Mats of stringy microbes float on cave pools. Globs of sticky microbes cling to the walls. Some microbes feed on sulfur minerals and limestone—they actually eat the walls of the cave! Then other microbes, and the cave's animals, eat them.

Working with Acid

As microbes nibble on the cave walls, they produce sulfuric acid. This dissolves the limestone and slowly makes the cave bigger. The same thing happens in many other caves all over the world. Their beautiful chambers and fairyland formations are carved partly by water and partly by rock-eating microbes.

Rock-eating microbes helped form Carlsbad Caverns in New Mexico (above).

In some caves, microbes make so much sulfuric acid that visitors have to wear acid-proof suits and masks. Without such protection, the cave air would burn their skin and dissolve the clothing off their backs.

Growing cave microbes in a lab can be tricky. Some of them make acid that's strong enough to dissolve lab equipment. Figuring out how to grow them in the lab may have huge benefits, though. Biologists have grown cave microbes that don't make acid. They've also discovered that some of them make chemicals that kill cancer cells.

A Risky Home

Not all cave critters love acid. Take bats, for instance. Some kinds of bats sleep in caves, hanging upside down from the ceiling. Whole colonies of bats have been killed in their sleep by a sudden gush of sulfuric acid. Their little bodies—or what's left of them—still cling to the cave ceiling.

Dig This

Scientists wondered if other life-forms lurked beneath Earth's surface. They thought that other incredible microbes might exist deep underground. Around the time Movile Cave was opened, the U.S. Department of Energy (DOE) drilled a hole 2 miles (3.2 km) deep in solid rock along the Columbia River in Washington State. DOE scientists were looking for helpful and harmful microbes. They thought they might unearth microbes that could help purify groundwater for drinking. Or they might find microbes that could damage the containers used to bury nuclear waste.

FUN FACT!

Just .04 ounce (1 g) of farm soil contains more than 1 billion bacteria. The same amount of rock contains only 100 to 10 million bacteria. But the total volume of rock in Earth's crust is so great that all the underground critters together might weigh more than all living things at the surface.

The DOE found microbes—lots of them. So did scientists studying other kinds of rock in other countries. Scientists have even discovered microbes more than 3 miles (1.9 km) deep in solid granite!

More than ten thousand kinds of rock "bugs" have been found so far. Most are bacteria or archaea. But fungi and other microbes live there too. And what do they live on, deep in their dark stony home? They eat rocks. Some underground microbes brought into a lab lived for a year, in a sealed chamber, on nothing but rocks and water!

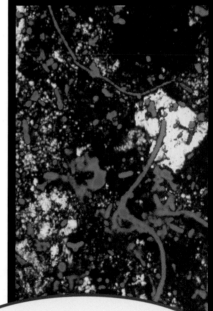

These rock-eating bacteria (red) were discovered inside rock more than 0.5 mile (0.8 km) below Earth's surface.

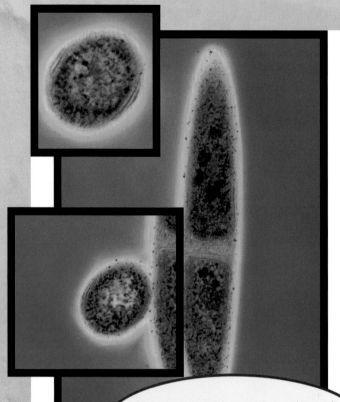

As the rock-eaters chow down, they make wastes that are eaten by other microbes. They also change the minerals around them. Some make methane, also known as natural gas. Many people use methane to heat their homes.

Other microbes make very pure deposits of metals. Microbes below ground in Nevada made a vein of zinc sulfide that weighs about 441,000 tons (400,000 metric tons). Zinc is a metal used in electronics, automobiles, and appliances. Some biologists think microbes made many of the pure mineral deposits on Earth.

Methanospirillum hungattii (above) is a microbe that lives without oxygen and produces methane gas.

Tasty Toxins

A home in solid rock looks cozy compared to the places we'll visit next. That is, unless you think of toxic waste as a gourmet meal.

You name it, something eats it—almost. So far, we don't know of anything that chows down on most plastics, detergents, or some pesticides. Other than that, anything goes. Soot, coal, kerosene, and ozone-depleting chemicals are all on the menu. And at least sixteen species of microbes use the common poison arsenic as their main source of energy!

The bad news about poison-eating microbes is that they often make as much poison as they eat. The bugs that eat soot off buildings and statues, for instance, also make acid that can damage those same buildings and statues.

Other microbes get their energy from the rocks, or tailings, that are left over after a mine is dug. That sounds harmless. But their waste products are acids and dissolved metals such as iron, copper, and zinc. The waste products pollute streams and groundwater near the tailings piles. The water becomes so toxic that it kills almost everything it touches. We can't drink it or put it on our crops. We can't even run it through a water treatment plant because it would corrode (break down) the pumps and pipes.

Lucky for us, not all toxin-eating bugs make things worse. Scientists have put many of them to work cleaning our water, air, and soil. Microbes digest oil spilled on water or land. A sewage-treatment plant in California uses bacteria to de-stink smelly water. Microbes even eat soil pollutants such as vinyl chloride and trichloroethane —toxic chemicals we once thought would stay in the ground forever.

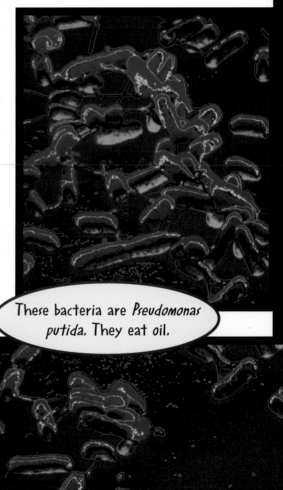

These bacteria are *Pseudomonas putida*. They eat oil.

Radiation Survivor

One microbe can survive radiation a thousand times stronger than the dose that kills a human being. Radiation is a form of energy that is released by chemical elements such as uranium and plutonium. It chops DNA into little pieces, which kills most organisms. But this talented microbe can repair the damage in less than twenty-four hours. If we could figure out how it does that, we might be able to cure human diseases that result from damaged DNA.

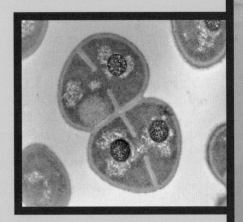

The bacterium Deinococcus radiodurans can survive a radiation dose 1,000 times greater than what is deadly to humans.

A Solution to Pollution?

If we can find microbes to eat so many kinds of pollution, why does our waste keep piling up? Because microbes can't do the whole job themselves. Take oil spills, for example. We can't just spray a microbe on them and say, "That's done." It takes many kinds of microbes to clean up oil, and we don't know much about any of them. Also, eating an oil slick takes weeks or months. While microbes munch their way through the goo, the oil that hasn't been eaten yet can still kill thousands of animals and plants.

Besides, we don't want oil-eating microbes to get out of control. What if they invaded oil fields? Or got into car engines? The same goes for other kinds of pollution and trash. To microbes, the things we want to keep can look just like the things we want to get rid of. Microbes can't tell the difference between an old computer and one that's still being used. Do we really want to find a microbe that devours steel and computer chips?

chapter 6

The Frontiers of Life

Extremophiles prove that organisms can live in environments hotter, colder, saltier, and darker than we ever imagined possible. They also give us a clue about how life might exist on other worlds. Thanks to thermophiles, we know that a boiling hot planet could harbor life. Thanks to rock-eating bugs, we know that a bare surface might hide a thriving underground community.

Welcome, Earthlings

The National Aeronautics and Space Administration (NASA) has projects to seek out signs of life on Mars and on Europa, one of Jupiter's moons. If we find living things on Mars or Europa, will they be related to Earth's extremophiles? It's possible. If they are related, they must have started out in the same place and somehow ended up on different planets. What if microbes hitched a ride on a meteor and brought life from one place to another?

Meteorites (pieces of rock) from Mars have landed on Earth many times. Maybe we'll find microbes on Mars that originally came from Earth. Or maybe microbes from Mars were the first organisms on Earth. Would that mean we're all Martians?

Scientists believe that this meteorite, known as ALH84001, came from Mars and fell to Earth about thirteen thousand years ago. Scientists once thought it contained evidence of life on Mars.

Space seems like the ultimate extreme environment. But we know that at least one Earth organism can survive it. When *Apollo 12* visited the Moon in 1969, its crew picked up a camera that had been left there two years earlier by an unmanned probe. Back on Earth, scientists opened the camera—and found a healthy colony of bacteria.

The Moon has extreme conditions, including blistering heat, freezing cold, no oxygen, and no water. But at least one microbe from Earth survived on the Moon for two years.

The bacteria were a species that normally lives in the human throat. That means someone working with the camera before the probe was launched probably coughed or sneezed on it. The bacteria aren't extremophiles, but they survived two years on the Moon! So maybe it's not such a wild idea that microbes might travel from planet to planet on meteorites.

What's Next?

Let's get back to what we actually know, which is constantly changing because new discoveries are made every day. Earth is probably home to thousands or millions more extremophiles that scientists haven't discovered yet. Any one of those species might change the way we think about life.

Every known living thing needs water in order to feed, grow, and reproduce. Water brings nutrients to cells, and it removes wastes. The chemical reactions that go on in living things cannot occur without water. Scientists look for evidence of water when looking for life.

But no matter what new things we learn, some things will still be true when you start making discoveries of your own. For instance, we know that life occurs almost everywhere on (and inside) Earth. If we haven't found living things in a certain place, it's probably because we haven't yet figured out how to keep them alive long enough to identify them.

Flaming Fireball

Things move fast in extreme research. Taq polymerase, the DNA profiling enzyme, has already been replaced in many labs. Pfu polymerase works at a higher temperature than Taq. It comes from a microbe that lives at hydrothermal vents and is named *Pyrococcus furiosus*, which means "flaming fireball."

Lake Vostok

Watch for news about Lake Vostok. That's a freshwater lake in Antarctica. It has been covered by 2.5 miles (4 km) of ice for millions of years. Scientists from many nations are working together to figure out how to get a sample of water from Lake Vostok without contaminating it with surface microbes. They want to find out whether the lake harbors life. But that's only one of their goals.

They also want to use this project as practice for a mission to Europa (above). Europa looks like it might be covered with water and ice. In other words, it looks like Lake Vostok. The probes we invent to visit Lake Vostok will help us plan our exploration of Europa.

All life-forms we know of need water. *Liquid* water. Evaporated water (water vapor) and frozen water (ice) won't do. That's why NASA spends so much time looking for traces of water on other planets. If a planet never had water, it probably never had life. If it did have water, then there's a good chance it was—or still is—home to living things.

That's about it. Everything else about life on the edge is waiting to be discovered. How extreme organisms got where they are, how they survive in conditions that would kill most creatures, what they can do for us—the big questions are still looking for answers. Whatever living things we find, in whatever weird environments, they will show us something new and unexpected about our amazing planet.

Glossary

antifreeze proteins (AFPs): proteins that slow the formation of ice in the body

archaea: a group of microbes thought to be the first forms of life on Earth. Archaea are like bacteria, but they have different genes and cellular structures.

bacteriorhodopsin: a protein, made by salt-loving microbes, that creates an electrical charge when it is struck by light

deoxyribonucleic acid (DNA): the molecule that carries genetic information

DNA profiling: a laboratory procedure that allows investigators to compare DNA samples from different sources

enzyme: a protein that makes a specific chemical reaction occur more quickly

extremophiles: organisms that thrive in conditions humans consider to be extreme

genes: sections of DNA that hold instructions for how to make specific proteins

halophiles: organisms that thrive in environments that are high in salt

heat shock proteins (HSPs): proteins made by cells in response to stresses such as high heat. HSPs make other proteins in a cell more stable.

hydrothermal vents: sites on the ocean floor at which ultrahot water and gases spew out of Earth's crust

hyperthermophiles: organisms that thrive at temperatures above 176°F (80°C)

membranes: flexible coverings of cells. They are made of fats, and they control what substances move into and out of cells.

microbes: organisms so small they can only be seen with a microscope. Bacteria and archaea are microbes.

polymerase: an enzyme that speeds the formation of new DNA strands

proteins: large molecules created according to instructions from genes. Proteins carry out all the processes of life, from making the hair on your head to breaking down the food in your stomach.

psychrophiles: organisms that thrive in cold environments

tailings: rock and metal ore left over after a mine is dug

thermal pools: ponds filled with water that was heated in Earth's crust. Thermal pools are sometimes called hot springs.

thermophiles: organisms that thrive at temperatures between 104°F (40°C) and 176°F (80°C)

Selected Bibliography

Books

Gross, Michael. *Life on the Edge: Amazing Creatures Thriving in Extreme Environments.* New York: Plenum Trade, 1998.

Howland, John L. *The Surprising Archaea: Discovering Another Domain of Life.* New York: Oxford University, 2000.

Postgate, John. *The Outer Reaches of Life.* Cambridge, UK: Cambridge University Press, 1994.

Rice, Tony. *Deep Ocean.* Washington, DC: Smithsonian Institute Press, 2000.

Robison, Bruce, and Judith Connor. *The Deep Sea.* Monterey, CA: Monterey Bay Aquarium Press, 1999.

Taylor, Michael Ray. *Dark Life: Martian Nanobacteria, Rock-eating Cave Bugs, and Other Extreme Organisms of Inner Earth and Outer Space.* New York: Scribner, 1999.

Van Dover, Cindy Lee. *The Octopus's Garden: Hydrothermal Vents and Other Mysteries of the Deep Sea.* Reading, MA: Addison-Wesley, 1996.

Wharton, David A. *Life at the Limits: Organisms in Extreme Environments.* Cambridge, UK: Cambridge University Press, 2002.

Interview

Dr. Kevin Humphries (head of the forensics laboratory of the Colorado Bureau of Investigation). April 30, 2004.

Further Reading and Websites

Archaea: The Extreme Microbes. http://www.microbeworld.org/htm/aboutmicro/ microbes/types/archaea.htm. This website features cool photos and weird facts about archaea and extremophiles.

Cerullo, Mary M. *Life Under Ice.* Gardiner, ME: Tilbury House, 2003. This book is filled with color undersea photographs that show animals in the waters of Antarctica.

Divining Water on Europa. http://science.nasa.gov/newhome/headlines/ast10dec99_2. htm. This NASA website includes the latest news about Lake Vostok and the search for life on other planets.

Fridell, Ron. *Decoding Life: Unraveling the Mysteries of the Genome.* Minneapolis: Lerner Publications Company, 2005. Discover the secrets of the genetic code that makes up all living things.

————. *Genetic Engineering.* Minneapolis: Lerner Publications Company, 2006. Learn more about the science of genetic engineering, including how scientists are changing plants and animals all around us.

Gowell, Elizabeth Tayntor. *Fountains of Life: The Story of Deep-Sea Vents.* New York: Franklin Watts, 1998. This book explains how hydrothermal vents formed and were discovered, and describes the creatures that live around them.

Hoyt, Erich. *Creatures of the Deep: In Search of the Sea's "Monsters" and the World They Live In.* Buffalo, NY: Firefly Books, 2001. This book features beautiful photos and tons of information about deep-sea creatures.

Jackson, Ellen, and Nic Bishop. *Looking for Life in the Universe.* Boston: Houghton Mifflin, 2002. This book describes the work of Dr. Jill Tarter, who is an astrophysicist and a research leader at an institute that looks for signs of life outside our planet.

Learn More. http://www.caves.org/committee/education/learnmoreaboutcaves.htm. Take a virtual tour of caves and find out more about cave life at this site sponsored by the National Speleological society.

Mallars, Neil. *Submarine.* New York: DK Publishing, 2003. Learn all about submarines and other underwater vessels.

Movile Cave. http://www.geocities.com/rainforest/vines/5771. This website has information about Movile Cave, its many strange creatures, and ongoing research there.

NOVA—Mysterious Life of Caves. http://www.pbs.org/wgbh/nova/caves/extremophiles. html. Hear from a biologist studying cave microbes and see a photo of snottites.

Pompeii Worm. http://www.ocean.udel.edu/extreme2002/creatures/pompeiiworm/. Meet the Pompeii worm and take a virtual tour of its habitat at this interactive website from the University of Delaware.

Seiple, Samantha, and Todd Seiple. *Mutants, Clones, and Killer Corn: Unlocking the Secrets of Biotechnology.* Minneapolis: Lerner Publications Company, 2005. This title provides an introduction to biotechnology, including its benefits, challenges, and controversies.

Winner, Cherie. *Cryobiology.* Minneapolis: Lerner Publications Company, 2006. Learn about the developing science of cryobiology and the animals and microbes that can survive in the coldest temperatures.

Index

About the Author

Cherie Winner holds a Ph.D. in zoology from Ohio State University. She is a full-time science writer for *Washington State Magazine.* Winner also writes books. Her published titles include *Salamanders, Coyotes, Trout, Woodpeckers, Erosion, Life in the Tundra,* and *Cryobiology.*

Photo Acknowledgments

The images in this book are used with the permission of: Michael Van Woert, NOAA NESDIS, ORA/NOAA corps collection, background image throughout; NASA/Jet Propulsion Laboratory, pp. 4, 39, 41; © Los Alamos National Laboratory/Photo Researchers, Inc., p. 5; © Kris Kuenning/National Science Foundation, p. 7; © Joe Tucciarone/Photo Researchers, Inc., p. 8; © C. Van Dover/OAR/National Undersea Research Program (NURP)/College of William and Mary, p. 9; © Dr. Dennis Kunkel/Visuals Unlimited, p. 10; © Dr. Gopal Murti /Visuals Unlimited, p. 12; © Sam Lund/Independent Picture Service, p. 13 (both); © Wolfgang Baumeister/Photo Researchers, Inc., p. 14; © SIU/Visuals Unlimited, p. 15; © Comstock Images, p. 16; © Jeffrey L. Rotman/CORBIS, p. 17; © Professor N. Russell/Photo Researchers, Inc., p. 18; © Paul A. Souders/CORBIS, p. 21 (left); © OAR/National Undersea Research Program (NURP)/Woods Hole Oceanographic Institute, p. 21 (right); © Norbert Wu/Peter Arnold, Inc., p. 22; © National Undersea Research Program (NURP) Collection, p. 23; © Mona Lisa Production/Photo Researchers, Inc., 24; © Lester V. Bergman/CORBIS, p. 26; © Richard T. Nowitz/CORBIS, p. 27; © Turbo/CORBIS, p. 28 (top); © A. B. Dowsett/ Photo Researchers, Inc., p. 28 (bottom); This image was made with VMD and is owned by the Theoretical and Computational Biophysics Group, an NIH Resource for Macromolecular Modeling and Bioinformatics, at the Beckman Institute, University of Illinois at Urbana-Champaign, p. 29; courtesy of the University of Cincinnati, p. 31; © David Muench/CORBIS, p. 32; T. Stevens and P. McKinley, Pacific Northwest Laboratory/Photo Researchers, Inc., p. 33; © Dr. Kari Lounatmaa/Photo Researchers, Inc., p. 34; © Manfred Kage/Peter Arnold, p. 35; © Peggy A. O'Gare, Margaret C. Henk, and John R. Battista, p. 36; NASA/ Photo Researchers, Inc, p. 38.; © Japack Company/CORBIS, p. 40.

Front cover: Michael Van Woert, NOAA NESDIS, ORA/NOAA corps collection (background); Peggy A. O'Gare, Margaret C. Henk, and John R. Battista (top right); Cristian Lascu (center); National Undersea Research Program (NURP) Collection /NOAA (bottom-right).